THE WEIRD A-COLORING TO AL

FELIPE SOBREIRO
WITH NATHAN RABIN

D1736829

The Weird A-Coloring to Al is adapted from The Weird Accordion to Al and The Weird Accordion to Al: The Ridiculously Self-Indulgent, Ill-Advised Vanity Edition, both of which can be purchased directly from the author at _www.nathanrabin.com/shop_

For more about "Weird Al" Yankovic, check out The Weird Accordion to Al and The Big Squeeze (_www.nathanrabin.com_) columns at Nathan Rabin's Happy Place and the 2012 coffee table book Weird Al: The Book (Rabin with Yankovic)

For more art by Felipe, check out his website at _www.sobreiro.com_

Special thanks to Mariana Rausch for doing an amazing job with the book design, Al Yankovic, Jon "Bermuda" Schwartz, Jay Levey, Scott Aukerman, Dr. Demento, Peyton Reed, Harris Wittels, The Onion, Andy Greene, The Long Shot, We Hate Movies, Laureane Sutir, Danya Maloon, Declan-Haven and Harris Theodore, Jason Webber, Insane Ian, Lauren Carey, the Maloon Family. Harvey Rabin, Matthew Chojnacki, 1984 Publishing, Steve Jay, Jim "Kimo" West, Rubén Valtierra, Harvey Rabin, Anna Rabin, Shari Lisa Rabin, Paul Degrassi, Clint Worthington, Dynasty Typewriter, Keith Phipps, Stephen Thompson, Eric Appel, Yacov Freedman, Z2, Ryan Britt, Daniel Radcliffe and Champion Simon of Dare to Dream, the best dog in the history of the universe and all of Al's Close Personal Friends and the "Weird Al" Yankovic fan community.

WELCOME TO THE GALA GRAND OPENING
OF THE *THIRD* ROCK AND ROLL HALL OF AL!

THE *FIRST* ROCK AND ROLL HALL OF AL HAD TO BE TORN DOWN BECAUSE LUNATICS KEPT COLORING ITS WALLS.

THIS WAS ILLEGAL AND VIOLATORS WERE ARRESTED AND/OR BEATEN SENSELESS BY POLICE.

THE *SECOND* ROCK AND ROLL HALL OF AL WAS NOT BIG ENOUGH TO HOUSE TWENTY NEW PORTRAITS SO IT WAS DESTROYED WITH DYNAMITE.

UNFORTUNATELY, THE MUSEUM WAS FULL OF FANS WHEN THE EXPLOSION OCCURRED.

THIRTY THOUSAND VISITORS WERE CRUSHED TO DEATH. EVEN MORE WERE BURIED ALIVE. THERE WERE BRAINS AND GUTS AND VITAL ORGANS SPLATTERED EVERYWHERE.

THE CARNAGE WAS NECESSARY TO CREATE A MUSEUM WORTHY OF CYNICALLY EXPLOITING THE HOT NEW BIOPIC *WEIRD: THE AL YANKOVIC STORY*.

ENJOY ALL THE NEW PORTRAITS AND TRY NOT TO LET THE ANGRY HOWLS OF THE DEAD RUIN YOUR CAREFREE GOOD TIME! WELCOME TO THE FUN ZONE!

Now Enter the Quiet Zone!! Pipe down or our head security guard Stanley will forcibly eject you. He used to work for Prince, so you know he means business!

"RICKY"

EVERY DAY'S A RERUN AND THE LAUGHTER'S ALWAYS CANNED.

"I LOVE ROCKY ROAD"

ALL THE SODA JERKERS KNOW HIS NAME.

THE CITY'S BIGGEST BOLOGNA BUYER.

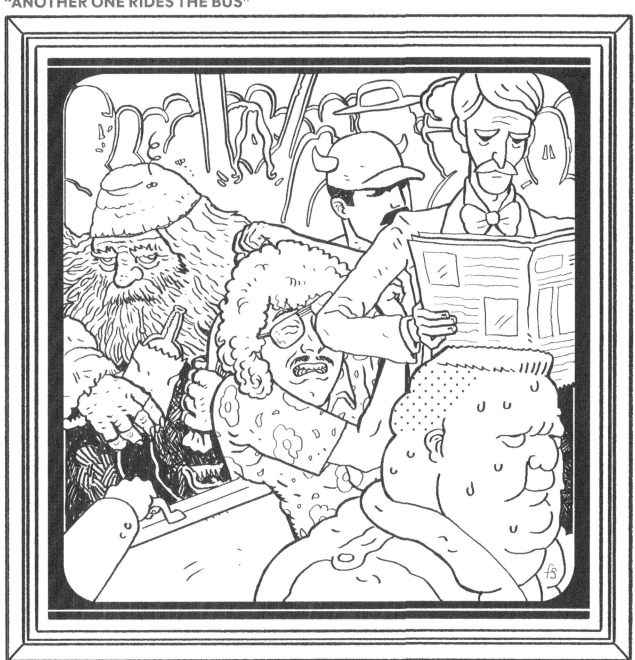

THE PUBLIC TRANSPORTATION ROUTE TO HELL IN 2-D.

"MR. FRUMP IN THE IRON LUNG"

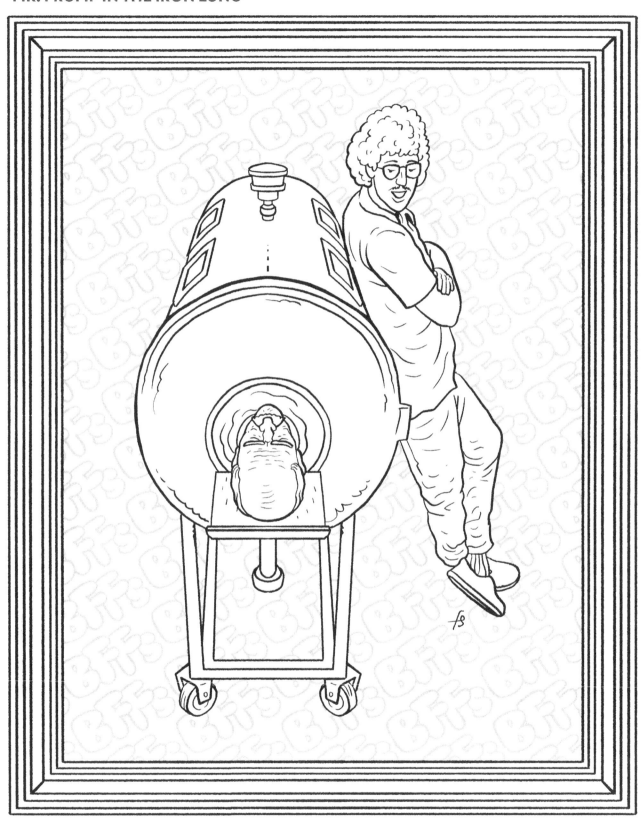

HONOR POOR MR. FRUMP'S DYING WISHES BY
COLORING IN HIS IRON LUNG **TASTEFULLY**!

"EAT IT"

"WEIRD AL" YANKOVIC, COLORING AND FOOD: CAN'T BEAT IT!

THE INCREDIBLE FROG BOY IS ON THE LOOSE AGAIN!

"THE BRADY BUNCH"

WHEN PENCILING IN THIS COLORFUL BUNCH
LET THE SCHWARTZ BE WITH YOU (BERMUDA **AND** SHERWOOD).

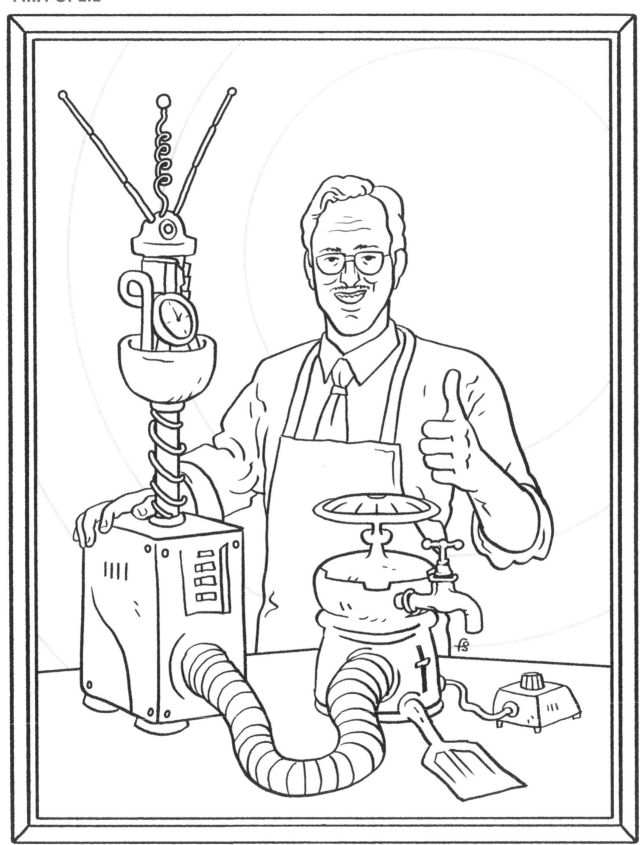

MR. POPEIL TO THE RESCUE!

DIAMOND JIM, THE EARLY YEARS.

"THE RYE OR THE KAISER (THEME FROM ROCKY XIII)"

A CHAMP AND HIS MEATS.

"NATURE TRAIL TO HELL"

.ZIHW ESEEHC STAE NATAS

"LIKE A SURGEON"

THE DISGRACE OF THE AMA!

ARE WE NOT MEN? WE ARE STUPID!

A MAGNIFICENT MALLARD.

"YODA"

THE JEDI TRAINING BEGINS.

"GEORGE OF THE JUNGLE"

WATCH OUT FOR THAT... **TREE!!!**

"SLIME CREATURES FROM OUTER SPACE"

THEY'RE NOT VERY NICE TO THE HUMAN RACE.

"THIS IS THE LIFE"

AL'S IN THE MONEY!

"LIVING WITH A HERNIA"

AL FEELS **BAD!!!**

"DOG EAT DOG"

STOP MAKING SENSE, START MAKING COPIES.

"ADDICTED TO SPUDS"

SOME TATER TOTS WOULD BLOW YOUR **MIND!**

"ONE OF THOSE DAYS"

EVER HAD ONE OF THOSE DAYS?

HE'S SUCH A COOL GUY!

"DON'T WEAR THOSE SHOES"

RANDOM FOOTWEAR FOR WAYWARD SOULS.

"TOOTHLESS PEOPLE"

HOW VILE!

GRIM NOEL.

"I THINK I'M A CLONE NOW"

CARBON COPY MEN.

"LASAGNA"

THE DAY THE MUSIC DINED.

"MELANIE"

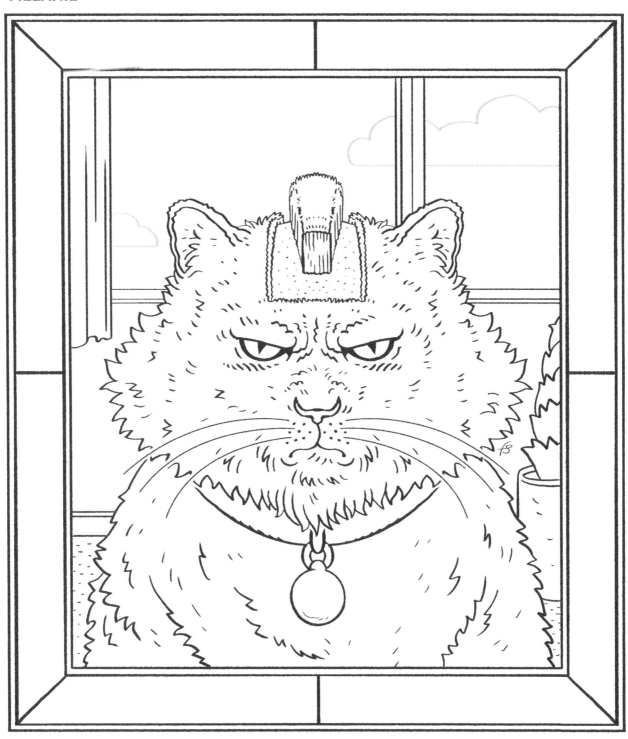

DISPLEASED FELINE.

THE KING OF VELVET.

"TWISTER"

BEASTIE BOY.

"GOOD OLD DAYS"

BRING BACK THE INNOCENT FUN OF YESTERYEAR BY
COLORING IN THIS ADORABLY TERRIFIED RODENT.

ELUSIVE TREASURE.

HE STARTS WHERE THE OTHERS STOP!

ELECTRIFYING CINEMA!

COLOR THIS KOOKY CULINARY CONCOCTION OF MEAT
AND SUGAR AND VARIOUS ENTRAILS!

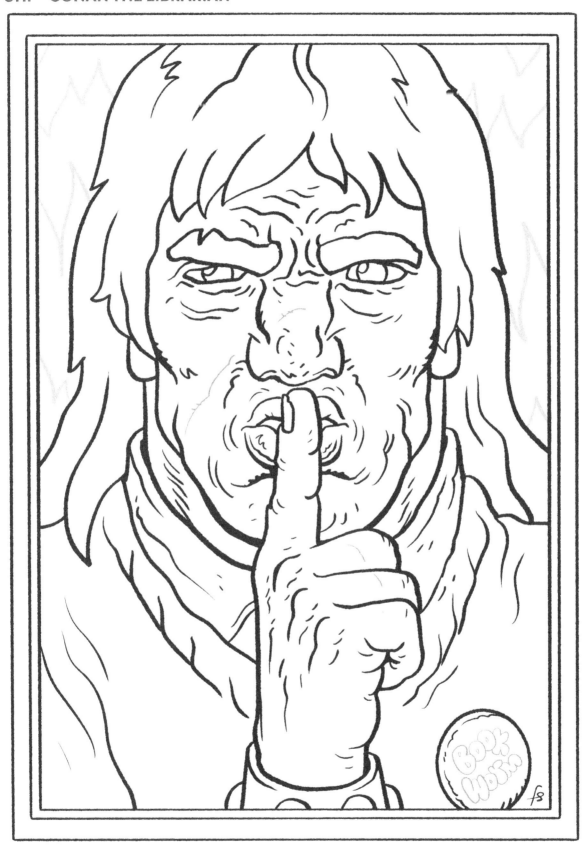

DON'T BE A BARBARIAN! RETURN YOUR LIBRARY BOOKS ON TIME AND FOR THE LOVE OF ALL THAT IS HOLY, **DO NOT COLOR THEM!**

"ATTACK OF THE RADIOACTIVE HAMSTERS FROM A PLANET NEAR MARS"

OBJECTS IN THE MIRROR ARE FORTY THOUSAND TIMES LARGER THAN THEY APPEAR.

CASTAWAYS CAPTIVATE!

"GENERIC BLUES"

AL IS THE CITY'S BIGGEST TOILET ROCKER!

"SPATULA CITY"

AT SPATULA CITY THEY SELL SPATULAS. AND THAT'S ALL!

"THE BIGGEST BALL OF TWINE IN MINNESOTA"

BEHOLD THE MAGNIFICENT MIDWESTERN ORB OF MAGIC AND MYSTERY!

SMELLS WEIRD, LIKE AL

"TRIGGER HAPPY"

THERE'S NO FEELING ANY GREATER THAN TO SHOOT FIRST AND ASK QUESTIONS LATER.

"THE WHITE STUFF"

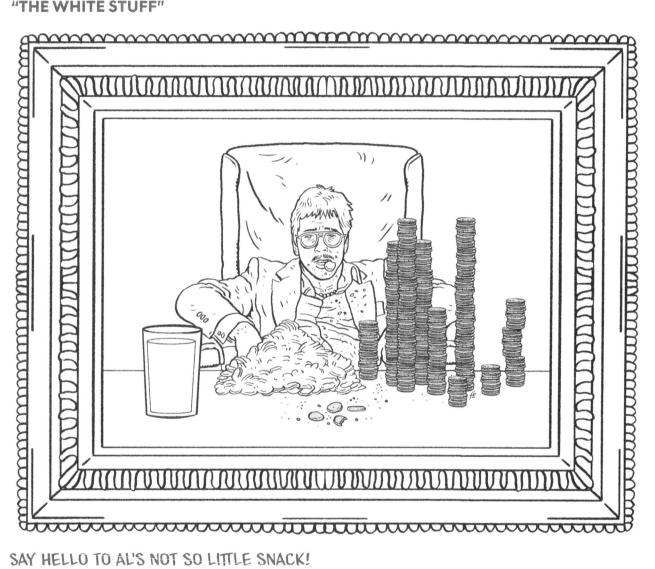

SAY HELLO TO AL'S NOT SO LITTLE SNACK!

"TACO GRANDE"

TACO TUESDAY TRIUMPHANT. GRANDE, GRANDE, GRANDE!

"THE PLUMBING SONG"

CALL THE MENSCH WITH A MONKEY WRENCH! HE'LL DO A SUPER JOB FOR YOU!

FOR THOSE ABOUT TO ANNOY (WE SALUTE YOU).

"BEDROCK ANTHEM"

JUST YABBA DABBA DO IT!

"FRANK'S 2000" TV"

IT DWARFS THE MIGHTY REDWOODS AND IT TOWERS OVER EVERYONE!

"ACHY BREAKY SONG"

AL WOULD RATHER HEAR SLIM WHITMAN OR ZAMFIR
THAN THAT STUPID SONG BY BILLY RAY.

"TALK SOUP"

HE WANTS TO TELL THE WORLD ABOUT IT!

YUCK IN A REFRIGERATOR!

"WAFFLE KING"

DO YOU **BELIEVE** IN THE **POWER** OF THE **WAFFLE**?

"BOHEMIAN POLKA"

IT'S WEIRD'S WORLD! IT'S WEIRD'S WORLD! PARTY TIME! EXCELLENT!

THE SHOCKING TRUTH! REVEALED FOR THE VERY FIRST TIME!

"CAVITY SEARCH"

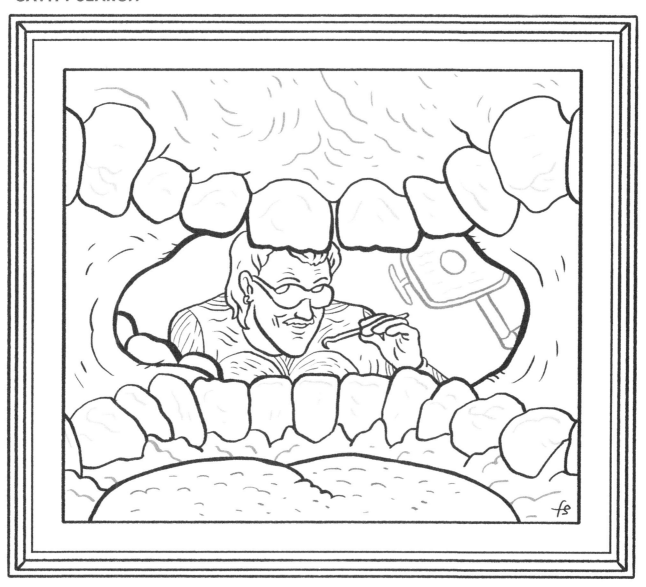

OPEN UP AND SAY AHHHHHHHHHHHHHHHHHHHH!!!!!!!!!!!!!!!!!!

"GUMP"

"MY NAME IS FORREST," HE'D CASUALLY REMARK.

"I REMEMBER LARRY"

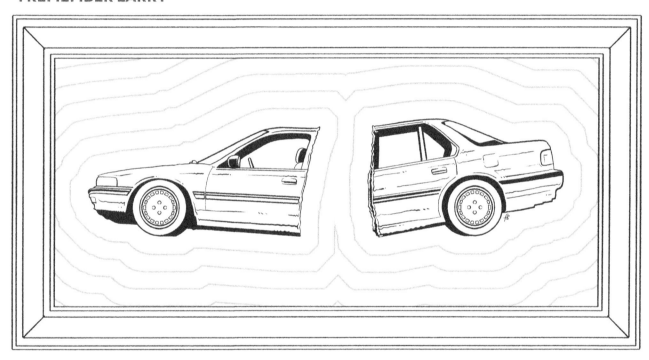

A PRETTY GOOD GAG.

"THE NIGHT SANTA WENT CRAZY"

GRIM NOEL, PART DEUX.

AMERICAN JAR JAR.

"MY BABY'S IN LOVE WITH EDDIE VEDDER"

SMELLS LIKE JEALOUSY.

"GERMS"

THE ENEMY UNSEEN!

"YOUR HOROSCOPE FOR TODAY"

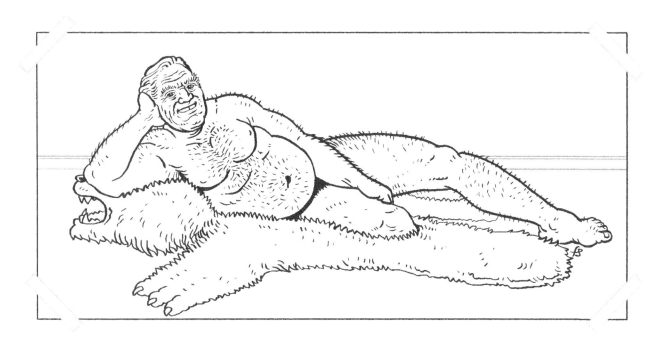

HANG UP THIS NAKED PICTURE OF ERNEST BORGNINE IN YOUR DEN.

"ALBUQUERQUE"

ALBUQUERQUE: WHERE THE SUN IS ALWAYS SHINING AND THE AIR SMELLS LIKE WARM ROOT BEER AND THE TOWELS ARE OH SO FLUFFY!

"COUCH POTATO"

WON'T THE REAL COUCH POTATO PLEASE SIT DOWN,
PLEASE SIT DOWN, PLEASE SIT DOWN?

"TRASH DAY"

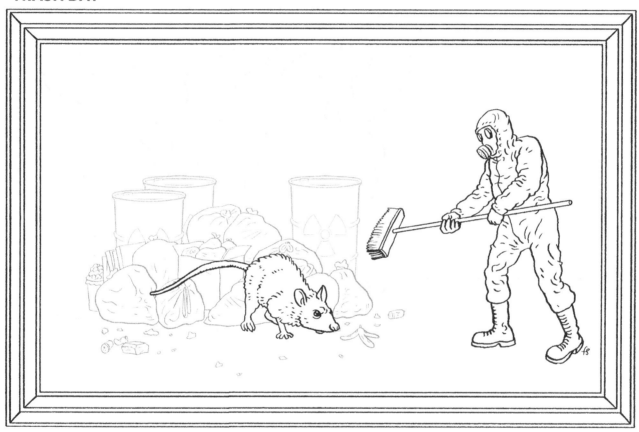

IT'S GETTING TRASHY IN HERRE!

"A COMPLICATED SONG"

A MAJOR INCONVENIENCE.

"ODE TO A SUPERHERO"

NOW PETER CRAWLS OVER EVERYONE'S WALLS AND HE'S SWINGIN' ALL OVER TOWN.

DETRITUS FROM A WORLDWIDE GARAGE SALE.

"WHITE & NERDY"

KIRK OR PICARD? THE ETERNAL DILEMMA.

"PANCREAS"

AL REALLY, **REALLY** LOVES HIS PANCREAS!

DON'T BE A PHONY BALONEY WHEN COLORING IN THIS NIFTY ZAMBONI!

RAGE IN A LITIGOUS AGE.

"VIRUS ALERT"

GRANNY'S SHOCKING DISCOVERY!

MAKE US PROUD BY COLORING IN THIS LOVE-STRUCK CREEP!

EXPRESS YOURSELF THROUGH COLORING! GO GAGA!

"CNR"

CHARLES NELSON REILLY WAS A MIGHTY MAN, THE KIND YOU NEVER DISRESPECT.

"CRAIGSLIST"

RED SPEEDO-WEARING, HOCKEY MASKED, SLIGHTLY SOILED SOMBRERO AND OLD WHEELBARROW OWNER LOOKING FOR LOVE AND/OR A 65 CHEVY MALIBU.

"ANOTHER TATTOO"

NOT JUST ANOTHER TATTOO.

YOU LIKE TOP RAMEN, NEED TOP RAMEN? GOT A CUPBOARD
FULL OF 'EM, I'LL KEEP 'EM COMIN'.

AFTER COLORING THIS IN, FORWARD A SCREENSHOT TO EVERYONE
YOU KNOW OR A DEAD GIRL WILL **DEFINITELY** KILL YOU.

"LAME CLAIM TO FAME"

LAME, FAMOUS (LEFT)

"FOIL"

AL HAS CRACKED THE CODE, HE'S FIGURED OUT THESE SHADOW ORGANIZATIONS.

DRUNKEN PRIEST, STOLEN ZEBRA.

"TACKY"

LIVE-TWEETING THE RECENTLY DECEASED.

ANOTHER ONE RIDES THE BUS.

"DR. DEMENTO JINGLE"

STAY DEMENTED!

"PAC-MAN"

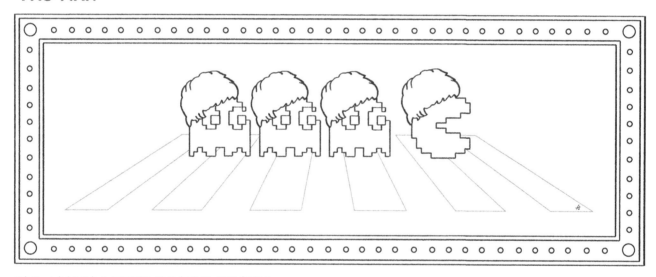

PAC-MANIA MEETS BEATLE FEVER!

MR. HAPPY HAS GONE MISSING.

"LOUSY HAIRCUT"

AL'S LOUSY NEW HAIRCUT IS QUITE THE CONVERSATION-STARTER!

"HOMER AND MARGE"

ANIMATED AL.

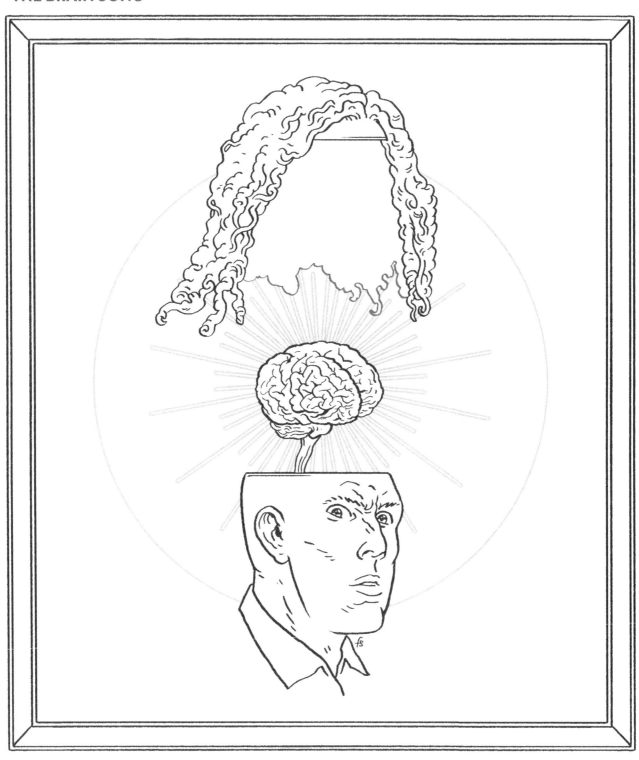

AL'S MIRACULOUS DETACHABLE CEREBELUM!

"COMEDY BANG! BANG! THEME"

INTERESTING TIMES.

SHIRLEY MACLAINE, PRE-REINCARNATION.

COLOR IN THIS YUPPIE GATOR, A LITTLE NOW AND A LITTLE LATER.

THE POODLE'S TRUE FORM.

"BEAT ON THE BRAT"

WITH A BRAT LIKE THAT ALWAYS ON YOUR BACK, WHAT CAN YOU LOSE?

"HAPPY BIRTHDAY"

IT WON'T BE LONG BEFORE WE'RE ALL GONNA DIE!

AL DURING THE ME, MYSELF AND I STAGE OF HIS CAREER.

THE PERILS OF PEER PRESSURE!

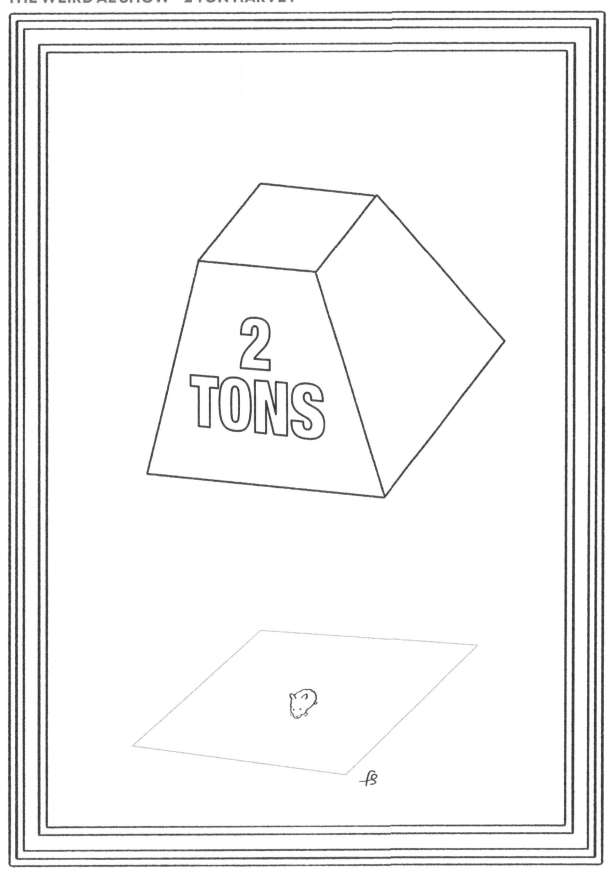

HARVEY IN DANGER!

RANDO!

THE ASTRONAUT ICE CREAM OF THE FUTURE: TODAY!

THE BOOLIES AND THE BANE OF THEIR EXISTENCE.

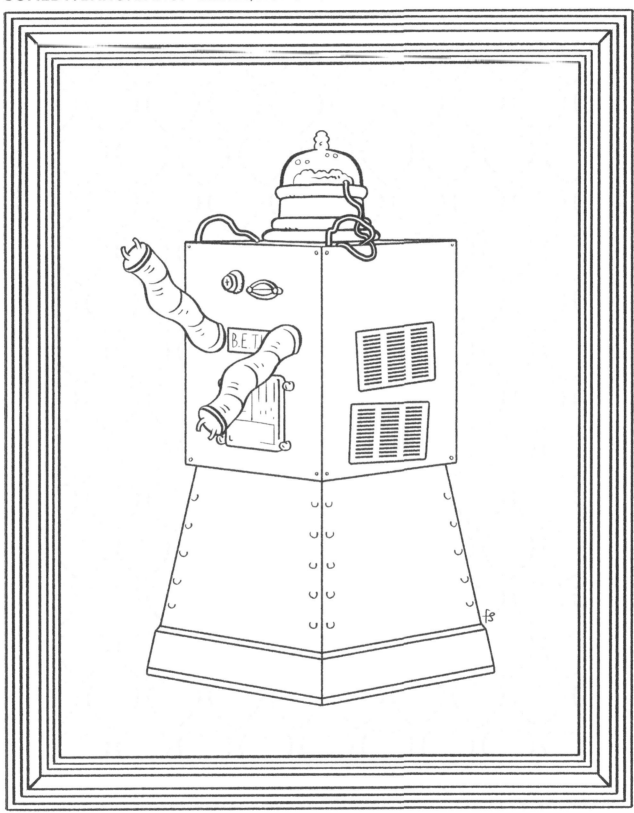

BLEEP BLOOP! B.E.T.H WAS MADE FOR LOVE AND HEARTBREAK!

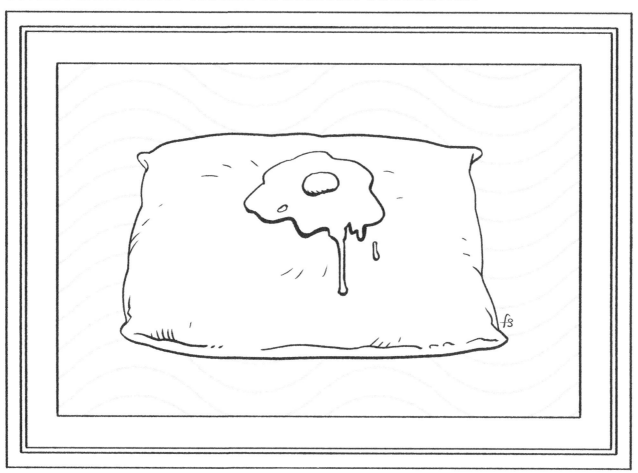

A GOOFY GOURMAND'S DELIGHT!

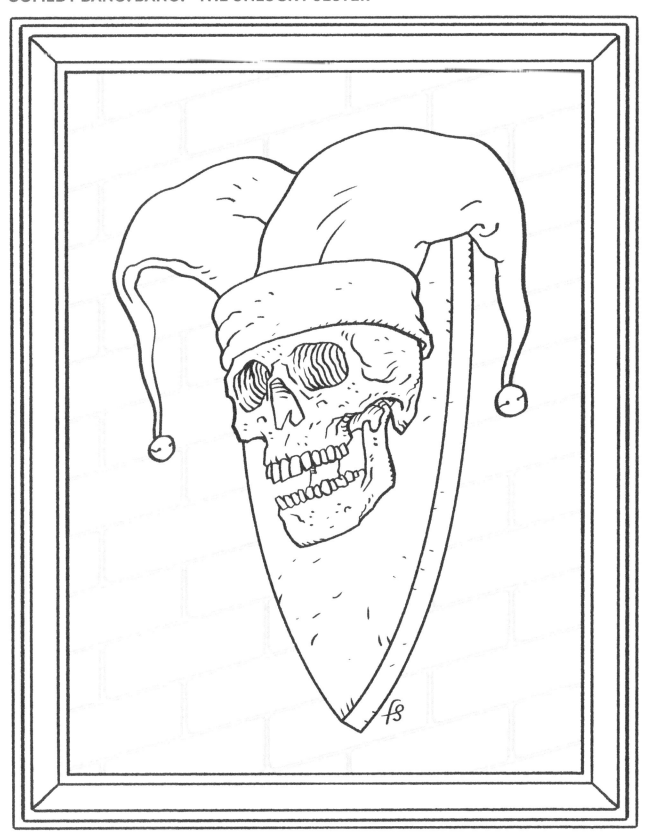

THE ULTIMATE PUNISHMENT.

TALL, DARK AND MENACING.

A HALLOWEEN TRICK.

THE HOMICIDAL HALLWAY.

SLOW JOEY IN HIS ELEMENT.

DON'T WASTE YOUR SHOT! GIVE THIS HIP HOP FOUNDING FATHER ALL YOU'VE GOT!

GET WEIRD WITH IT, YOU COLORING WIZARD!

AL AND ASSOCIATE.

THANKS FOR VISITING THE ROCK AND ROLL HALL OF AL.

COME BACK THE NEXT TIME AL DOES SOMETHING BIG AND WE'LL
BE HAPPY TO TAKE MORE OF YOUR HARD-EARNED CASH!

Made in the USA
Monee, IL
12 April 2023

31756279R00070